THE

SANDY FOUNDATION SHAKEN:

TO WHICH IS ADDED,

INNOCENCY WITH HER OPEN FACE,

BY WAY OF APOLOGY.

———ooo———

BY WILLIAM PENN,

A builder on that foundation which cannot be moved;

———ooo———

TRENTON:

FRANCIS S. WIGGINS, PRINTER.

1827.

TO THE

UNPREJUDICED READER.

———

IT was the fault of some in ancient times, that they
made void God's law by men's traditions; and certainly I may now assume the same complaint. For
whilst I take a serious prospect of the spiritual nature
and tendency of the second covenant, which God Almighty, in the fulness of time, by his prophets, pro-
phesied to make and perfect; and also the accomplishment thereof by Jesus Christ, and what was brought
to pass amongst the primitive believers; methinks I
do not only see an utter abolishment of ceremonial
worships, but the inscribing that spiritual law on the heart,
and infusion of holy fear to the inward parts, whereby
each person became capacitated to know so much of
God, as suited with his present state, from an infalliable demonstration in himself, and not on the slender
grounds of man's lo-here interpretations, or lo-there:
for the kingdom of God is within, where himself must
be the teacher of his people. But on the other hand,
when from the noise of ever party's pretensions to,
and contentions for their own way, as most infalliable,
I am induced to an impartial examination of them;
alas! how have all adulterated from the purity both
of scripture record, and primitive example! receiving
for unquestionable doctrines, the falliable apprehensions,

and uncertain determinations of such councils, whose faction, prejudice, and cruelty soon paralleled the foregoing heathenish persecutions. And yet that the results of persons so incompetently qualified, should at this day in their authority remain unquestioned by the nations, is matter both of astonishment and pity. But an implicit faith has ever been the consequence of ignorance, idleness, and fear, being strong impediments to a judicious inquiry, how far professed and imposed opinions have their consistency with reason, and the true religion. But that which most of all deserves a lamentation, is, that Protestants, whose better arguments have confuted the plea of such as made tradition, and men's prescriptions unquestionble in circumstantials, should themselves, by print and practice, so openly declare and contend for its authority in essentials; as must be obvious to any that observe their zealous anathemas against whomsoever refuse a compliance with them in doctrines, manifestly bottomed upon men's nice inventions.

This is the right state of the controversy that is maintained by us, contemptibly called Quakers, against the world, and the undoubted reason of our severe treatment at its hands. The end of God Almighty's raising us, being for no other purpose, than to declare "that which our eyes have seen, our ears heard, and which our hands have handled of the eternal word," in opposition to the private opinions, conjectures, and interpretations of men concerning God and religion, that all people might thereby be reduced to faith in, and obedience to, the universal grace which brings salvation; which as it only can restore sound judgment concerning God, and effect redemption from iniquity, so its being relinquished by men, was the very ground both of their division in judgment, and corruption in manners.

That this has been, and is our case, I shall produce an instance, which is indeed the occasion of this teatise.

Two persons lately of Thomas Vincent's auditory in Spittle-Fields, (who goes under the notion of a Presbyter), being desirous to prove all things, and to hold fast the best, visited our meeting, to understand if we were as really deserving blame, as represented by our enemies; where it then pleased divine goodness to visit them with the call of his Light, from the inventions, carnal observations, will-worship, and vain conversation of those to whom they were formerly related, that they might be made children of the day. And though its appearance might be small, yet sufficient to discover them to have been inhabitants of the night, and can never be rejected, but it shall bring that condemnation which will further testify it to be of God.

But their relinquishing his congregation, so incensed this Presbyterian preacher, that his peevish zeal transported him beyond, not only the moderation of christianity, but the civility of education, venting his folly and prejudice much to this purpose : " That he had as lieve they should go to a bawdy-house, as to frequent the Quakers' meetings, because of their erroneous and damnable doctrines." And pointing to the window, said : " If there should stand a cup of poison, I would rather drink it, than suck in their damnable doctrines." He further expressed himself in this manner to one of them : " If ever you go again, I will give you up, and God will give you up, that you may believe a lie, and be damned." Which storms of foul and railing accusations, proving ineffectual to shipwreck that little grain of faith, his hearers, as forgetting they hold their preaching by connivance, and the many appeals made by their non-conforming brethren, for an indulgence, came with this caution to the *pater-familias*, (or he that was both husband and father to the concerned parties), that he would exercise his authority, as well to refuse them to all Quaker visitants, as prohibit them the liberty of their consciences in frequenting our meetings.

All which we could not for the truth's sake, let pass in silence, and therefore did require him to let us have a public meeting, in which we might have liberty to answer on the behalf both of ourselves and principles which after some demur, was granted, the day he appointed, and at the second hour in the afternoon. But that he might not want the applause of many voices, and doubtless to prevent our friends, as, I am informed, bespoke his usual auditory to be there at one. And, as a man that would not overspend himself, or incur a a non-plus for want of seconds, he had his third and fourth, to wit, Thomas Danson, Thomas Doolittle, and ——— Maddocks, who at their times (and often out of them) did interpose, to whom George Whitehead mostly answered; nor had there any thing been spoken by another, but from their own example.

The matter in controversy, will be related in the beginning of this treatise, as a necessary preludium, or introduction to the following discourse. The manner of it was so gross, that I know not how to represent it better, than by the levity and rudeness of some prize; laughing, hissing, shoving, striking, and stigmatizing us with the opprobious terms of " confident fellow," " impudent

villian," "blasphemer," &c. And, as the usual refuge of
shallow persons, when they have little else to say, to pre-
possess their hearers with prejudice against the principles
of such as oppose them, he questioned much whether I
was not some Jesuit; not remembering, or at least unwilling to let the people know, that none have been, nor are
more instant in the vindication of that doctrine he and
his brother did assert, to wit, God subsisting in three
distinct persons, than the Jesuits. So that if I should
not as well reflect a scandal upon their learning by a
comparison, as he did upon my principle, I could more
truly invert "Jesuitism" upon himself. In short, they
neither would keep to scripture terms themselves, nor
suffer it in others. But looking upon George Whithead's
explanation of their terms, and reduction of their matter, (if possible), to a scripture sense, thereby fitting it
to the auditors' apprehension, to be an indirect way of
answering, (as that which nakedly exposed their tra-
ditional folly to the vulgar), Thomas Vincent, in an
abrupt manner, fell to his prayer, in which he falsely,
and with many strangely affected whines, accused us
for blasphemers unto God. And that he might prevent the clearing of ourselves, he desired the people,
when he had finished, to be gone, giving them an example by his and three brethren's retreat. But we being desirous further to inform the people of our innocency, they did not only (as before) endeavor to pull
us down, but put the candles out, though several persons, of good esteem, continued whilst we spoke in
vindication of ourselves, from the invectives of our adversaries.

The people still remaining undispersed, Thomas
Vincent came very palely down the stairs, having a

candle in his hand, requiring their dismission, at which time he promised us, at our request, another meeting. But as one that knew not well what he said, or never purposed to perform what he promised, he has given us since to understand, he cannot in conscience spare us so much time; yet to satisfy George Whitehead and myself, in private, he could agree; which surely cannot be termed another meeting, since then it must relate to the preceding one. But how near the relation is betwixt an accusation before hundreds, and a satisfaction before none, must needs be obvious to every unbiassed person.—Our right should have been altogether as public as our wrong.—For which cause we were necessitated to visit his meeting, where, on a lecture day, after a continued silence during all his worship, we modestly intreated we might be cleared from those unjust reflections before his congregation, leaving a disputation, if he could not then attend it, to some more seasonable opportunity. But as one, who resolved injustice to men's reputation, as well as cowardice, in baulking a defence of his own principles, he slunk most shamefully away; nor would any there, though urged to it, assume his place to vindicate his practice towards us, or his doctrines then delivered.

Reader, what is thy opinion of this savage entertainment? Would Socrates, Cato or Seneca, whom they call heathens, have treated us with such unseemly carriage? I suppose not. And well is it for the truly sober and conscientious, they are not liable to those severe lashes, and that peevish usage, which are the inseparable appendix to a Scotch directory, whose cold and cutting gales ever have designed to nip and blast the fairest blossoms of greater reformation. So much for history.

What remains, is to inform the reader, that with great brevity 1 have discussed, and endeavored a total enervation òf those cardinal points, and chief doctrines so firmly believed, and continually imposed for articles of christian faith: 1. The trinity of seperate persons, in the unity of essence. 2. God's incapacity to forgive, without the fullest satisfaction paid him by another. 3. A justification of impure persons, from an imputative.righteousness. Which principles let me tell thee, reader, are not more repugnant to scripture, reason, and souls-security, than most destructive to God's honor, in his unity, mercy, and purity.

Therefore I beseech thee to exterminate passion from her predominancy, in the perusal of this abridged discourse, since it was written in love to thee; that whilst it is thy desire to know, love, and fear God Almighty above men's precepts, thou. mayest not miss so good an end, by the blind embraces of tradition for truth. But in the nobility of a true Berean, search and inquire ; letting the good old verity, not a pretended antiquity, (whilst a mere novelty), and solid reason, not an overfond credulity, sway the balance of thy judgment, that both stability and certainty may accompany thy determinations. Farewell.

A short Confutation by way of Recapitulation, of what was objected against us at Thomas Vincent's meeting.

If disputations prove at any time ineffectual, it is either to be imputed to the ignorance and ambiguity of the disputants, or to the rudeness and prejudice of

2

the auditory. All which may be truly affirmed of Thomas Vincent with his three brethren, and congregation.

The accusation being general, viz. "That the Quakers held damnable doctrines:" George Whitehead on their behalf stood up, and as it was his place, willingly would have given the people an information of our principles, which if objected against, he was as ready to defend them by the authority of scripture and reason. But instead of this better method, Thomas Vincent, as one that is often employed in catechistical lectures, falls to interrogatories, begging that himself, he in his slander had taken for granted, to wit, the knowledge of our principles.

The question was this: "Whether we owned one God-head, subsisting in three distinct and separate persons," as the result of various revises and amendments. Which being denied by us, as a doctrine no where scriptural, Thomas Vincent frames this sillogism from the beloved desciple's words.

"There are three that bear record in heaven, the Father, the Word, and the Holy Ghost; and these three are one."—1 John v..7.

"These are either three manifestations, three operations, three substances, or three somethings else beside subsistences.

"But they are not three minifestations, three operations, three substances, nor three somethings else beside subsistences:

Ergo, Three subsistences."

George Whitehead utterly rejected his terms, as not to be found in scripture, nor deducible from the place he instanced. Wherefore he desires their explanation of their terms, inasmuch as God did not use to wrap his truths up in heatheni-h metaphysics, but in plain language. Notwithstanding we could not obtain a bet- ter explication than *person*, nor of person, than the mode of substance. To all which George Whitehead and myself urged several scriptures, proving God's complete unity. And when we queried how God was to be understood, if in an abstractive sense· from his substance; they concluded it a point more fit for ad- miration than disputation. But a little to review his syllogism. The manner of it shews him as little a scholar, as its matter does a christian. But I shall over-look the first, and so much of the second, as might deserve my objection to his major, and give in short my reason, why I flatly deny his minor proposition. No one substance can have three distinct subsistences, and preserve its own unity. For granting them the most favorable definition, every subsistence will have its own substance; so that three distinct subsistences, or manners of being, will require three distinct sub- stances or beings; consequently three Gods. For if the infinite God-head subsists in three separate manners. or forms, then is not any one of them a perfect and complete subsistence without the other two; so parts, and something finite is in God. Or if infinite, then three distinct infinite subsistences; and what is this but to assert three Gods, since none is infinite but God? And on the contrary, there being an inseparability betwixt the substance and its subsistence, the unity of substance will not admit a trinity of incommunicable or distinct subsistences.

Thomas Danson being asked "Of whom was Christ the express image?" from his alleging that scripture in the Hebrews; answered: "Of God's subsistence, or manner of being." From whence two things in short follow as my reply: It makes God a Father only by subsistence, and Christ a Son without a substance. Besides it is falsely rendered in the Hebrews, since the Greek does not say KARAKTER PROOSPOU, but KARAKTER TES UPOSTASEOS, the character of substance.

And if he will persue a farther discovery of his error, and explanation of the matter, let him read Col. i. 15. "Who is the image of the invisible God." Heb. i. 3.

And because George Whitehead, willing to bring this strange doctrine to the capacity of the people, compared their three persons to three apostles, saying, he did not understand how Paul, Peter, and John could be three persons, and one apostle, (a most apt comparison to detect their doctrine), one ———— Maddocks, whose zeal out-stript his knowledge, bustling hard, as one that had some necessary matter for the decision of our controversy, instead thereof, (perhaps to save his brethren, or show himself), silences our farther controverting of the principle, by a sollogistical, but impertinent reflection upon George Whitehead's person. It runs thus: " He that scornfully and reproachfully compares our doctrine of the blessed trinity of Father, Son, and Spirit, one in essence, but three in persons, to three finite men, as Paul, Peter, and John, is a blasphemer. But you George Whitehead have so done. *Ergo.*"

A strange way of argumentation, to beg what cannot be granted him, and take for granted what still remains a question, viz. "That there are three distinct and separate persons in one essence." Let them first prove their trinity, and then charge their blasphemy.

But I must not forget this person's self-confutation, who to be plainer, called them three "*He's*," and if he can find an *He* without a substance, or prove that a subsistence is any other than the form of an *He*, he would do well to justify himself from the imputation of ignorance.

And till their hypothesis be of better authority, George Whitehead neitheir did, nor does by that comparison design men's invention so much honor.

For it is to be remarked, that George Whitehead is no otherwise a blasphemer, than by drawing direct consequences from their own principles, and recharging them upon themselves. So that he did not speak his own apprehensions by his comparison, but the sense of their assertion; therefore blasphemer and blasphemy are their own.

————

The trinity of distinct and separate persons, in the unity of essence, refuted from scripture.

"And he said Lord God, there is no God like unto thee." Kings viii. 23.—"To whom then will ye liken me, or shall I be equal? saith the Holy One." Isa. xl. 25.—"I am the Lord, and there is none else, there is no God besides me." ch. xlv. 5. "Thus saith the Lord, thy Redeemer, the Holy One of Israel." ch. xlviii. 17.—"I will also praise thee, O my God; unto thee will I sing, O Holy One of Israel." Psal. lxxi. 22,—"Jehovah shall be One, and his name One." Zec. xiv. 9.—Which with a cloud of other testimonies that might be urged, evidently demonstrate, that in the days of the first covenant, and prophets, but One was the Holy God, and God but that Holy One.—Again: "And Jesus said unto him, Why callest thou me good? There is none good but One, and that is God." Mat. xix. 17.—" And this is life eternal, that they might know thee (Father) the only true God." John xvii. 3.—"Seeing it is One God that shall justify." Rom. iii. 30.— "There be gods many—but unto us there is but One God, the Father, of whom are all things." 1 Cor. viii. 6.—" One God and Father who is above all things." Eph. iv. 6.—" For there is One God." 1 Tim. ii. 5. " To the only wise God be glory now and ever." Jude ver. 25.—From all which I shall lay down this one assertion, that the testimonies of scripture, both under the law, and since the gospel dispensation, declare One to be God, and God to be One, on which I shall raise this argument:

If God, as the scriptures testify, hath never been declared or believed, but as the Holy One, then will it follow, that God is not an Holy Three, nor doth subsist in three distinct and separate Holy Ones. But the before-cited scriptures undeniably prove that One is God, and God only is that Holy One. Therefore he cannot be divided into, or subsist in an Holy Three, or three distinct and separate Holy Ones. Neither can this receive the least prejudice from that frequent but impertinent distinction, that he is one in substance, but three in persons or subsistences: since God was not declared or believed incompletely, or without his subsistence. Nor did he require homage from his creatures, as an incomplete or abstract being, but as God the Holy One: for so he should be manifested and worshipped without that which was absolutely necessary to Himself.—So that either the testimonies of the aforementioned scriptures are to be believed concerning God, that he is entirely and completely, not abstractly and distinctly, the Holy One, or else their authority to be denied by these trinitarians. And on the contrary, if they pretend to credit those holy testimonies, they must necessarily conclude their kind of trinity a fiction.

Refuted from right reason.

1. If there be three distinct and separate persons, then three distinct and separate substances, because every person is inseparable from its own substance; and as there is no person that is not a substance in common acceptation among men, so do the scriptures plentifully agree herein; and since the father is God, the son is God, and the spirit is God (which their opinion necessitates them to confess) then unless the father, son and spirit, are three distinct nothings, they must be three distinct substances, and consequently three distinct Gods.

2. It is farther proved, if it be considered, that either the divine persons are finite or infinite; if the first, then something finite is inseparable to the infinite substance, whereby something finite is in God; if the last, then three distinct infinites, three omnipotents, three eternals, and so three Gods.

3. If each person be God, and that God subsists in three persons, then in each person are three persons or Gods, and from three, they will increase to nine, and so ad infinitum.

4. But if they shall deny the three persons, or substances to be infinite, (for so there would unavoidably

be three Gods) it will follow that they must be finite,
and so the absurdity is not abated from what it was;
for that of one substance having three subsistences, is
not greater, than that an infinite being should have
three finite modes of subsisting. But though that mode
which is finite cannot answer to a substance that is infinite; yet to try if we can make their principle to consist, let us conceive that three persons, which may be
finite separately, make up an infinite conjunctly; however this will follow, that they are no more incommunicable or separate, nor properly subsistences, but a subsistence; for the infinite substance cannot find a bot-
tom or subsistence in any one or two, therefore jointly.
And here I am also willing to overlook finiteness in
the father, son and spirit, which this doctrine must suppose.

5. Again, if three distinct persons are one, with some
one thing, as they say they are with the Godhead, then
are not they incommunicable among themselves; but
so much the contrary, as to be one in the place of another: for if that the only God is the father, and Christ
be that only God, then is Christ the father. So if that
one God be the son, and the spirit that one God, then is
the spirit the son, and so round. Nor is it possible to
stop, or that it should be otherwise, since if the divine
nature be inseparable from the three persons, or communicated to each, and each person have the whole divine nature, then is the son the father, and the spirit in
the son, unless that the Godhead be as incommunicable
to the persons, as they are reported to be amongst themselves; or that the three persons have distinctly allot-
ted them such a proportion of the divine nature, as is
not communicable to each other; which is alike absurd.

Much more might be said to manifest the gross contra-diction of this trinitarian doctrine, as vulgarly received; but I must be brief.

Information and Caution.

Before I shall conclude this head, it is requisite I should inform thee, reader, concerning its original; thou mayest assure thyself, it is not from the scriptures, nor reason, since so expressly repugnant; although all broachers of their own inventions strongly endeavor to reconcile them with that holy record. Know then, my friend, it was born above three hundred years after the ancient gospel was declared; and that through the nice distinctions, and too daring curiosity of the bishop of Alexandria, who being as hotly opposed by Arius, their zeal so reciprocally blew the fire of contention, animos-ity and persecution, till at last they sacrificed each oth-er to their mutual revenge.

Thus it was conceived in ignorance, & brought forth and maintained by cruelty; for though he that was strongest imposed his opinion, persecuting the contra-ry, yet the scale turning on the trinitarian side, it has there continued through all the Romish generations; and not withstanding it has obtained the name of Athanasian from Athanasius, (a stiff man, witness his carriage towards Constantine the emperor) because sup-posed to have been most concered in the framing that creed in which this doctrine is asserted; yet have I never seen one copy void of a suspicion, rather to have been the results of popish school men; which I could render more perspicuous, did not brevity necessitate me to an omission.

Be therefore cautioned, reader, not to embrace the

...r evangelical ... lent to certain testi... ...the primitive saints ...in the first, sec... Ireneus, Justin ... others who ... controversy.—... ...one of the most ...and guardians of the ...time past suf... ...mind to that ...that by obedi... ...hath east before ...receive a certain ...is life eternal, ...and eternal be... ...his son, as ...light which enlighteneth every man; that who-soever followed him (the light) might be translated from the dark notions, and vain conversations of men, to this holy light, in which only sound judgment and eternal life are obtainable; who so many hundred years since, in person, testified the virtue of it, and has communicated unto all such a proportion, as may enable them to follow his example.

The vulgar doctrine of satisfaction, being dependent on the second person of the trinity, refuted from scripture.

DOCTRINE.—" That man having transgressed the righteous law of God, and so exposed to the penalty of eternal wrath, it is altogether impossible for God to remit or forgive without a plenary satisfaction; and that there was no other way by which God could obtain satisfaction, or save men, than by inflicting the penalty of infinite wrath and vengeance on Jesus Christ the second person of the trinity, who for sins past, present and to come, hath wholly borne and paid it [whether for all, or but some], to the offended infinite justice of his Father."

REFUTATION.—1. "And the Lord passed by before him [Moses], and proclaimed, the Lord, the Lord God, merciful and gracious, keeping mercy for thousands, forgiving iniquity, transgression and sin." Exod. xxxiv. 6, 7.—From whence I shall draw this position, that since God has proclaimed himself a gracious, merciful, and forgiving God, it is not inconsistent with his nature to remit, without any other consideration than his own love : otherwise he could not justly come under the imputation of so many gracious attributes, with whom it is impossible to pardon, and necessary to exact the payment of the utmost farthing.]

2. "For if ye turn again to the Lord, the Lord your God is gracious and merciful, and will not turn away his face from you."—2. Chron. xxx, 9. Where how natural is it to observe that God's remission is grounded on their repentance ; and not that it is impossible for God to pardon without plenary satisfaction, since the possibility, nay, certainty of the contrary, viz. his grace and mercy, is the great motive, or reason, of that loving invitation to return.

3. "They hardened their necks, and hearkened not to thy commandments; but thou art a God ready to pardon, gracious and merciful." Neh. ix. 15, 1

the honest hearted reader conceive, that God should thus be mercifully qualified, whilst executing the rigor of the law transgressed, or not acquitting without the debt be paid him by another? I suppose not.

4. "Let the wicked forsake his way, and the unrighteous man his thoughts, and let him return unto the Lord, and he will have mercy upon him, and to our God, for he will abundantly pardon." Isaiah lv. 7.—Come, let the unprejudiced judge, if this scripture doctrine is not very remote from saying his nature cannot forgive sin, therefore let Christ pay him full satisfaction or he will certainly be avenged; which is the substance of that strange opinion.

5. "Behold the days come, saith the Lord, that I will make a new covenant with the house of Israel; I will put my law in their inward parts; I will forgive their iniquity, and I will remember their sin no more." Jer. xxxi. 31, 33, 34.—Here is God's mere grace asserted, against the pretended necessity of a satisfaction to procure his remission. And this Paul acknowledgeth to be the dispensation of the gospel, in his eighth chapter to the Hebrews. So that this new doctrine, doth not only contradict the nature and design of the second covenant, but seems, in short, to discharge God, both from his mercy and omnipotence.

6. "Who is a God like unto thee, that pardoneth iniquity, and passeth by the transgressions of the remnant of his heritage? He retaineth not his anger for ever, because he delighteth in mercy." Micha vii. 18. —Can there be a more express passage to clear, not only the possibility, but real inclination in God to pardon sin, and *not retain his anger for ever;* since the prophet seems to challenge all other gods, to try their

excellency by his God Herein describing the supremacy of his power, and super-excellency of his nature, that "he pardoneth iniquity, and retaineth not his anger for ever." So that if the satisfactionists should ask the question, who is a God like unto ours, that cannot pardon iniquity, nor pass by transgression, but retaineth his anger until somebody make him satisfaction? I answer, many amongst the harsh and severe rulers of the nation; but as for my God, he is exalted above them all, upon the throne of his mercy, "who pardoneth iniquity, and retaineth not his anger for ever, but will have compassion upon us."

7. "And forgive us our debts, as we forgive our debtors." Mat. vi. 12.—Where nothing can be more obvious, than that that which is forgiven, is not paid. And if it is our duty to forgive our debtors, without a satisfaction received, and that God is to forgive us, as we forgive them, then is a satisfaction totally excluded. Christ farther paraphrases upon that part of his prayer, v. 14. "For if ye forgive their trespasses, your Heavenly Father will also forgive you." Where he as well argues the equity of God's forgiving them, from their forgiving others, as he encourages them to forgive others, from the example of God's mercy, in forgiving them. Which is more amply expressed, ch. xviii. where the kingdom of heaven (that consists in righteousness), is represented by a king, "who, upon his debtors petition, had compassion, and forgave him; but the same treating his fellow-servant without the least forbearance, the king condemned his unrighteousness, and delivered him over to the tormentors." But how had this been a fault in the servant, if his king's mer-

cy had not been proposed for his example? How most unworthy therefore is it of God, and blasphemous, may I justly term it, for any to dare to assert that forgiveness is impossible to God, which is not only possible, but enjoined to men.

8. "For God so loved the world, that he gave his only begotten Son, that whosoever believeth in him should not perish, but have everlasting life." John iii. 16.—By which it appears, that God's love is not the effect of Christ's satifaction, but Christ is the proper gift and effect of God's love.

9. "To him give all the prophets witness, that through his name, whosoever believeth in him, shall receive remission of sins." Acts x. 43.—So that *remission* came by believing his testimony, and obeying his precepts, and not by a strict satisfaction.

10. "If God be for us, who can be against us? He that spared not his own Son, but delivered him up for us all." Rom. viii. 31, 32.—Which evidently declares it to be God's act of love, otherwise, if he must be paid, he should be at the charge of his own satisfaction, for he delivered up the Son.

11. "And all things are of God, who hath reconciled us to himself by Jesus Christ, and hath given-to us the ministry of reconciliation, to wit, that God was in Christ, reconciling the world to himself, not imputing their trespasses unto them." 2. Cor. v. 18, 19.—How undeniably apparent is it, that God is so far from standing off in high displeasure, and upon his own terms, contracting with his Son for a satisfaction, as being otherwise incapable to be reconciled, that he became himself the reconciler by Christ, and afterwards by the apostles, his ambassadors, to whom was committed the ministry of reconciliation.

12. "In whom we have redemption through his blood, the forgiveness of sins, according to the riches of his grace." Eph. i. 7.—Now what relation, satisfaction has to forgiveness of sins, or how any can construe grace to be strict justice, the meanest understanding may determine.

13. "But the God of all grace, who hath called us unto his eternal glory, by Christ Jesus." 1 Pet. v. 10.—He does not say that God's justice, in consideration of Christ's satisfaction, acquitted us from sins past, present, and to come, and therefore hath called us to his eternal glory; but from his grace.

14. "In this was manifest the love of God towards us, because that God sent his only begotten Son into the world, that we might live through him." 1 John. iv. 9.—Which plainly attributes Christ in his doctrine, life, miracles, death, and sufferings, to God, as the gift and expression of his eternal love, for the salvation of men.

1. In abolishing that other covenant, which consisted in the external and shadowy ordinances, and that made none clean as concerning the conscience.

2. In promulgating his message, of a most free and universal tender of life and salvation, to all that believed and followed him, (the Light), in all his righteousness; the very end of his appearance being to destroy the works of the devil, and which every man only comes to experience, as he walks in an holy subjection to that measure of light and grace, wherewith the fulness hath enlightened him.

3. In seconding his doctrines with signs, miracles, and a most innocent self-denying life.

4. In ratifying and confirming all, (with great love

and holy resignation), by the offering up of his body, to be crucified by wicked hands: who is now ascended far above all heavens, and is thereby become a most complete captain, and perfect example.

So that I can by no means conclude, but openly declare, that the scriptures of truth, are not only silent in reference to this doctrine of rigid satisfaction, but that it is altogether inconsistent with the dignity of God, and very repugnant to the conditions, nature, and tendency of that second covenant, concerning which their testimony is so clear.

The absurdities, that unavoidably follow the comparison of this doctrine, with the sense of scripture.

1. That God is gracious to forgive, and yet it is impossible for him, unless the debt be fully satisfied.

2. That the finite and impotent creature, is more capable of extending mercy and forgiveness, than the infinite and omnipotent Creator.

3. That God so loved the world, he gave his only begotten Son to save it; and yet that God stood off in high displeasure, and Christ gave himself to God as a complete satisfaction to his offended justice. With many more such like gross consequences that might be drawn.

Refuted from right reason.

But if we should grant a scripture silence, as to the necessity of Christ's so satisfying his Father's justice; yet so manifest would be the contradictions, and foul

the repugnancies to right reason, that he who had not
veiled his understanding with the dark suggestions of
unwarrantable tradition, or contracted his judgment to
the implicit apprehensions of some over-valued ac-
quaintance, might with great facility discriminate to a
full resolution in this point. For admitting God to
be a creditor, or he to whom the debt should be paid,
and Christ he that satisfies or pays it on the behalf of
man, the debtor, this question will arise, whether he
paid that debt, as God, or man, or both? (to use their
own terms.)

Not as God.

1. In that it divides the unity of the God-head, by
two distinct acts, of being offended, and not offended;
of condemning justice and redeeming mercy; of requiring a satisfaction, and then making it.

2. Because if Christ pays the debt as God, then the
Father and the Spirit being God, they also pay the
debt.

3. Since God is to be satisfied, and that Christ is
God, he consequently is to be satisfied; and who shall
satisfy his infinite justice?

4. But if Christ has satisfied God the Father, Christ
being also God, it will follow then that he has satisfied himself, which cannot be.

5. But since God the Father was once to be satisfied, and that it is impossible he should do it himself,
nor yet the Son or Spirit, because the same God; it
naturally follows, that the debt remains unpaid, and
these satisfactionists thus far are still at a loss.

Not as man.

6. The justice offended being infinite, his satisfaction ought to bear a proportion therewith, which Jesus Christ, as man, could never pay, he being finite, and from a finite cause, could not proceed an infinite effect; for so man may be said to bring forth God, since nothing below the divinity itself, can rightly be styled infinite.

Not as God and man.

7. For where two mediums, or middle propositions, are singly inconsistent with the nature of the end for which they were at first propounded, their conjunction does rather augment than lessen the difficulty of its accomplishment. And this, I am persuaded, must be obvious to every unbiassed understanding.

But admitting one of these three mediums possible for the payment of an infinite debt ; yet, pray observe the most unworthy and ridiculous consequences, that unavoidably will attend the impossibility of God's pardoning sinners without a satisfaction.

Consequences irreligious and irrational.

1. That it is unlawful and impossible for God Almighty to be gracious and merciful, or to pardon transgressors ; than which, what is more unworthy of God.

2. That God was inevitably compelled to this way of saving men ;—the highest affront to his incontrollable nature.

3. That it was unworthy of God to pardon, but not to inflict punishment on the innocent, or require a satisfaction where there was nothing due.

4. It doth not only disacknowledge the true virtue and real intent of Christ's life and death, but entirely deprives God of that praise which is owing to his greatest love and goodness.

5. It represents the Son more kind and compassionate than the Father. Whereas, if both be the same God, then either the Father is as loving as the Son, or the Son as angry as the Father.

6. It robs God of the gift of his Son for our redemption, (which the scriptures attribute to the unmerited love he had for the world), in affirming the Son purchased that redemption from the Father, by the gift of himself to God, as our complete satisfaction.

7. Since Christ could not pay what was not his own, it follows that in the payment of his own, the case still remains equally grevious; since the debt is not hereby absolved or forgiven, but transferred only; and by consequence we are no better provided for salvation than before, owing that now to the Son which was once owing to the Father.

8. It no way renders man beholding, or in the least obliged to God, since by their doctrine he would not have abated us, nor did he Christ, the last farthing, so that the acknowledgments are peculiarly the Son's; which destroys the whole current of scripture testimony, for his good will towards men.—Oh! the infamous portraiture this doctrine draws of the Infinite Goodness! Is this your retribution, O injurious satisfactionists?

9. That God's justice is satisfied for sins past, present, and to come; whereby God and Christ have lost both their power of enjoying godliness, and prerogative of punishing disobedience. For what is once paid,

is not revokable; and if punishment should arrest any for their debts, it either argues a breach on God's, or Christ's part, or else that it has not been sufficiently solved, and the penalty completely sustained by another: forgetting, " that every one must appear before the judgment seat of Christ, to receive according to the things done in the body." 2 Cor. v. 10.—Yea, "every one must give an account of himself to God." Rom. xiv. 12.—But many more are the gross absurdities and blasphemies that are the genuine fruits of this so confidently believed doctrine of satisfaction.

A CAUTION.

Let me advise, nay, warn thee, reader, by no means to admit an entertainment of this principle, by whomsoever recommended; since it does not only divest the glorious God of his sovereign power, both to pardon and punish, but as certainly insinuates a licentiousness, at least a liberty that unbecomes the nature of that ancient gospel once preached among the primitive saints, and that from an apprehension of a satisfaction once paid for all. Whereas, I must tell thee, that unless thou seriously repent, and no more grieve God's holy spirit placed in thy inmost parts, but art thereby taught to deny all ungodliness, and led into all righteousness; at the tribunal of the Great Judge thy plea shall prove invalid, and thou receieve thy reward without respect to any other thing than the deeds done in the body. "Be not deceived, God will not be mocked; such as thou sowest, such shalt thou reap." Gal. vi. 7.; which leads me to the consideration of my third head, viz. justification by an imputative righteousness.

Justification of impure persons, by an imputative righteousness, refuted from scripture.

DOCTRINE. " That there is no other way for sinners to be justified in the sight of God, than by the imputation of that righteousness of Christ, long since performed personally; and that sanctification is consequential, not antecedent."

REFUTATION. 1. " Keep thee far from a false matter; and the innocent and righteous slay thou not; for I will not justify the wicked." Ex. xxiii. 7. Whereon I ground this argument, that since God has prescribed an inoffensive life, as that which can only give acceptance with him, and on the contrary hath determined never to justify the wicked, then will it necessarily follow, that unless this so much believed imputative righteousness, had that effectual influence, as to regenerate and redeem the soul from sin, on which the malediction lies, he is as far to seek for justification as before. For whilst a person is really guilty of a false matter, I positively assert from the authority and force of this scripture, he cannot be in a state of justification. And as God will not justify the wicked, so by the acknowledged reason of contraries, the just he will never condemn, but they, and they only, are the justified of God.

2. " He that justifieth the wicked, and he that condemneth the just, even they both are an abomination to the Lord." Prov. xvii. 15. It would very opportunely be observed, that if it is so great an abomination in men to justify the wicked, and condemn the just, how much greater would it be in God, which this doctrine of imputative righteousness necessarily does imply, that so far disengages God from the person justi-

fied, as that his guilt shall not condemn him, nor his innocency justify him? But will not the abomination appear greatest of all, when God shall be found condemning of the just, on purpose to justify the wicked, and that he is thereto compelled, or else no salvation; which is the tendency of their doctrine, who imagine the righteous and merciful God, to condemn and punish his innocent Son, that he having satisfied for our sins, we might be justified (whilst unsanctified) by the imputation of his perfect righteousness. Oh! Why should this horrible thing be contended for by christains?

3. " The son shall not bear the iniquity of his father; the righteousness of the righteous shall be upon him, and the wickedness of the wicked shall be upon him. When a righteous man turneth away from his right-eousness, for his iniquity that he hath done shall he die." Again: " When the wicked man turneth away from his wickedness, and doeth that which is lawful and right, he shall save his soul alive; yet saith the house of Israel, the ways of the Lord are not equal: are not my ways equal!" Ezek. xviii. 20, 26, 27, 29. If this was once equal, it is so still, for God is unchangeable: and therefore I shall draw this argument, that the condemnation or justification of persons, is not from the imputation of another's righteousness, but the actual performance and keeping of God's righteous statutes or commandments; otherwise God should forget to be equal. Therefore how wickedly unequal are those, who *not from scripture evidences, but their own dark conjectures and interpretations of obscure passages,* would frame a doctrine so manifestly inconsistent with God's most pure and equal nature; making

im to condemn the righteous to death, and justify
he wicked to life, from the imputation of another's
ighteousness : a most unequal way indeed.

4. " Not every one that saith unto me Lord, Lord,
shall enter into the kingdom of heaven, but he that doth the will of my Father." " Whosoever heareth these
ayings of mine, and doeth them, I will liken him unto
a wise man which built his house upon a rock," &c.
Mat. vii. 21, 24, 25. How very fruitful are the scrip-
ures of truth, in testimonies against this absurd and
dangerous doctrine. These words seem to import a
twofold righteousness, the first consists in sacrifice, the
ast in obedience. The one makes a *talking*, the other
a *doing* christian. I in short argue thus : If none can
enter into the kingdom of heaven, but they that do the
Father's will, then none are justified, but they who do
he Father's will, because none can enter into the king-
lom, but such as are justified. Since, therefore, there can
be no admittance had, without performing that righteous will, and doing those holy and perfect sayings;
alas ! to what value will an *imputative righteousness*
amount, when a poor soul shall awake polluted in its
sin, by the hasty calls of death, to make its appearance
before the judgment seat, where it is impossible to justify the wicked, or that any should escape uncondemn-
ed, but such as do the will of God.

5. " If ye keep my commandments, ye shall abide
in my love, even as I have kept my Father's commandments, and abide in his love." John. xv. 10. From
whence this argument doth naturally arise. If none are
truly justified that abide not in Christ's love, and that
none abide in his love, who keep not his commandments, then consequently none are justified but such as
keep his commandments. Besides, here is the most pal-

pable opposition to an imputative righteousness that
may be. For Christ is so far from telling them of such
a way of being justified, that he informs them the reason
why he abode in his Father's love, was his obedience;
and is so far from telling them of their being justified,
whilst not abiding in his love, by virtue of his obedience
imputed to them, that unless they keep his commands,
and obey for themselves they shall be so remote from
an acceptance, as wholly to be cast out:—in all which
Christ is our example.

6. " Ye are my friends, if ye do whatsoever I com-
mand you." John xv. 14. We have almost here the
very words, but altogether the same matter, which af-
fords us thus much, without being Christ's friends there
is no being justified. But unless we keep his commandments, it is impossible we should be his friends; it
therefore necessarily follows, that except we keep his
commandments, there is no being justified. Or, in
short thus: If the way to be a friend, is to keep the
commandments, then the way to be justified is to keep
the commandments, because none can obtain the quali-
ty of a friend, and remain unjustified, or be truly justified, whilst an enemy, which he certainly is, that keeps
not the commandments.

7. " For not the hearers of the law are just before
God, but the doers of the law shall be justified." Rom.
ii. 13. From whence how unanswerably may I observe
unless we become doers of that law, which Christ came
not to destroy, but, as our example, to fulfil, we can
never be justified before God. Wherefore obedience
is so absolutely necessary, that short of it there can be
no acceptance. Nor let any fancy that Christ hath so
fulfilled it for them, as to exclude their obedience from
being requisite to their acceptance, but as their pattern;

'for unless ye follow me,' saith Christ, 'ye cannot be
my disciples.' And it is not only repugnant to reason,
but in this place particularly refuted; for if Christ had
fulfilled it on our behalf, and we not enabled to follow
his example, there would not be doers, but one doer
only of the law justified before God. In short, if without obedience to the righteous law none can be justified,
then all our hearing of the law, with but the mere imputation of another's righteousness, whilst we are actually breakers of it, is excluded, as not justifying before
God. 'If you fulfil the royal law, ye do well; so speak
ye, and so do ye, as they that shall be judged' thereby.

8. "If ye live after the flesh, ye shall die; but if ye
through the spirit, do mortify the deeds of the body,
ye shall live." Rom. viii. 13. No man can be dead,
and justified before God, for so he may be justified that
lives after the flesh; therefore they only can be justified that are alive. From whence this follows, if the
living are justified and not the dead, and that none can
live to God, but such as have mortified the deeds of
the body through the spirit, then none can be justified
but they who have mortified the deeds of the body
through the spirit. So that justification does not go before, but is subsequential to the mortification of lusts,
and sanctification of the soul, through the spirit's operation.

9. "For as many as are led by the spirit of God, are
the sons of God." Rom. viii. 14.—How clearly will it
appear to any but a cavilling and tenacious spirit, that
man can be no farther justified, than as he becomes obedient to the spirit's leadings. For if none can be a son
of God, but he that is led by the spirit of God, then
none can be justified without being led by the spirit of

6

God, because none can be justified but he that is a son of God. So that the way to justification and son-ship, is through obedience to the spirit's leadings, that is, manifesting the holy fruits thereof by an innocent life and conversation.

10. "But let every man prove his own work, and then shall he have rejoicing in himself alone, and not in another." "Be not deceived, for whatsoever a man soweth, that shall he reap." Gal. vi. 4, 7.—If rejoicing and acceptance with God, or the contrary, are to be reaped from the work that a man soweth, either to the flesh or to the spirit, then is the doctrine of acceptance and ground of rejoicing, from the works of another, utterly excluded, every man reaping according to what he hath sown, and bearing his own burden.

11. "Was not Abraham our father justified by works, when he had offered Isaac his son upon the altar? Ye see then how that by works a man is justified, and not by faith only." Jam. ii. 21, 24.—He that will seriously peruse this chapter, shall doubtless find some, to whom this epistle was wrote, of the same spirit with the satisfactionists and imputarians of our time, they fain would have found out a justification from faith in the imputation of another's righteousness. But James, an apostle of the Most High God, who experimentally knew what true faith and justification meant, gave them to understand from Abraham's self-denying example, that unless their faith, in the purity and power of God's grace, had that effectual operation to subdue every beloved lust, wean from every Delilah, and entirely to resign and sacrifice Isaac himself, their faith was a fable, or as a body without a spirit. And as righteousness, therefore, in one person cannot justify another from unrigh-

teousness, so whoever now pretend to be justified by
faith, whilst not led and guided by the spirit into all
the ways of truth, and works of righteousness, their
faith they will find at last a fiction.

12. "Little children, let no man deceive you, he
that doeth righteousness, is righteous, as God is righteous, (but) he that committeth sin is of the devil." 1
John iii. 7, 8.—From whence it may be very clearly
argued, that none can be in a state of justification, from
the righteousness performed by another imputed to
them, but as they are actually redeemed from the commission of sin. For, if, 'he that committeth sin is of
the devil,' then cannot any be justified completely before God, who is so incompletely redeemed, as yet to
be under the captivity of lust, since then the devil's
seed, or offspring may be justified; but that is impossible. It therefore follows, that as he who doeth righteousness, is righteous, as God is righteous; so no farther is he like God, or justifiable. For in whatsoever
he derogates from the works of that faith, which is held
in a pure conscience, he is no longer righteous or justified, but under condemnation as a transgressor, or dis-
obedient person to the righteous commandment. And
if any would obtain the true state of justification, let
them circumspectly observe the holy guidings and in-
structions of that unction, to which the apostle recommended the ancient churches, that thereby they may
be led out of all ungodliness, into truth and holiness;
so shall they find acceptance with the Lord, who has
determined, "never to justify the wicked."

Refuted from right reason.

1. Because it is impossible for God to justify that which is both opposite and destructive to the purity of his own nature, as this doctrine necessarily obliges him to do, in accepting the wicked, as not such, from the imputation of another's righteousness.

2. Since man was justified before God, whilst in his native innocency, and never condemned till he had erred from that pure state; he never can be justified, whilst in the frequent commission of that for which the condemnation came. Therefore to be justified, his redemption must be as entire as his fall.

3. Because sin came not by imputation, but actual transgression; for God did not condemn his creature for what he did not, but what he did; therefore must the righteousness be as personal for acceptance, otherwise these two things will necessarily follow: First, That he may be actually a sinner, and yet not under the curse. Secondly, That the power of the first Adam to death, was more prevalent than the power of the second Adam to life.

4. It is therefore contrary to sound reason, that if actual sinning brought death and condemnation, any thing besides actual obedience unto righteousness, should bring life and justification. For death and life, condemnation and justification, being vastly opposite, no man can be actually dead and imputatively alive. Therefore this doctrine, so much contended for, carries this gross absurditiy with it, that a man may be actually sinful, yet imputatively righteous; actually judged and condemned, yet imputatively justified and glorified. In short, he may be actually damned, and yet

imputatively saved; otherwise it must be acknowledged, that obedience to justification ought to be as personally extensive, as was disobedience to condemnation. In which real, not imputative sense, those various terms of sanctification, righteousness, resurrection, life, redemption, justification, &c. are most infallibly to be understood.

5. Nor are those words, *impute, imputed, imputeth, imputing*, used in scripture by way of opposition, to that which is actual and inherent, as the assertors of an imputative righteousness do by their doctrine plainly intimate; but so much the contrary, as that they are never mentioned, but to express men really and personally to be that which is imputed to them, whether as guilty, as remitted, or as righteous. For instance: " What man soever of the house of Israel, that killeth an ox, and bringeth it not to the door of the tabernacle, to offer unto the Lord, blood shall be imputed unto that man." Lev. xvii. 3, 4.—or charged upon him as guilty thereof.—" And Shimei saith unto the king, let not my Lord impute iniquity unto me, for thy servant doth know that I have sinned." 2. Sam. xix. 18, 19, 20.

6. " But sin is not imputed where there is no law." Rom. v. 13. From whence it 'is apparent that there could be no imputation, or charging of guilt upon any, but such as really were guilty. Next, it is used about remission: " Blessed is the man unto whom the Lord imputeth not iniquity." Psal. xxxii. 2.—or as the foregoing words have it, ' whose transgression is forgiven.' Where the non-imputation doth not argue a non-reali-

7

ity of sin, but the reality of God's pardon; for otherwise there would be nothing to forgive, nor yet a real
pardon, but only imputative, which according to the
sense of this doctrine, I call imaginary. Again: 'God
was in Christ reconciling the world unto himself, not
imputing their trespasses unto them.' 2 Cor. v. 19.—
Where also non-imputation, being a real discharge for
actual trespasses, argues an imputation, by the reason of
contraries, to be a real charging of actual guilt. Lastly,
it is used in relation to righteousness. 'Was not Abraham justified by works when he offered Isaac? And
by works was faith made perfect, and the scripture was
fulfilled, which saith, Abraham believed God, and it was
imputed unto him for righteousness.' Jam. ii. 21, 22,
23.—By which we must not conceive, as do the dark
imputarians of this age, that Abraham's offering personally was not a justifying righteousness, but that God
was pleased to account it so; since God never accounts
a thing that which it is not. Nor was there any imputation of another's righteousness to Abraham, but on the
contrary, his personal obedience was the ground of that
just imputation. And therefore that any should be justified from the imputation of another's righteousness,
not inherent, or actually possessed by them, is both ridiculous and dangerous. Ridiculous, since it is to say
a man is rich to the value of a thousand pounds, whilst
he is not really or personally worth a groat, from the
imputation of another who has it all in his possession.
Dangerous, because it begets a confident persuasion in
many people of their being justified, whilst in captivity
to those lusts, whose reward is condemnation. Whence
came that usual saying amongst many professors of religion, that God looks not on them as they are in them-

selves, but as they are in Christ. Not considering that none can be in Christ, who are not new creatures, which those cannot be reputed, who have not disrobed themselves of their old garments, but are still enmantled with the corruptions of the old man.

Consequences irreligious and irrational.

1. It makes God guilty of what the sctiptures say is an abomination, to wit, that he justifieth the wicked.

2. It makes him look upon persons as they are not, or with respect, which is unworthy of his most equal nature.

3. He is hereby at peace with the wicked, (if justified whilst sinners), who said, ' there is no peace to the wicked.'

4. It does not only imply communion with them here, in an imperfect state, but so to all eternity, for 'whom he justified, them he also glorified.' Rom. viii. 30.—Therefore whom he justified whilst sinners, them he also glorified whilst sinners.

5. It only secures from the wages, not the dominion of sin, whereby something that is sinful comes to be justified, and that which defileth, to enter God's kingdom.

6. It renders a man justified and condemned, dead and alive, redeemed and not redeemed at the same time, the one by an imputative righteousness, the other a personal unrighteousness.

7. It flatters men, whilst subject to the world's lusts, with a state of justification, and thereby invalidates the very end of Christ's appearance, which was to destroy the works of the devil, and take away the sins of the

world; a quite contrary purpose than what the satisfactionists, and imputarians of our times have imagined,
viz: to satisfy for their sins, and by his imputed righteousness, to represent them holy in him, whilst unho-
ly in themselves. Therefore since it was to take away
sin, and destroy the devil's works, which were not in
himself, for that Holy One saw no corruption, conse-
qently in mankind; what can therefore be concluded
more evidently true, than that such in whom sin is not
taken away, and the devil's works undestroyed, are
strangers, notwithstanding their conceits, to the very
end and purpose of Christ's manifestation.

Conclusion, by way of caution.

Thus, reader, have I led thee through those three so
generally applauded doctrines, whose confutation I
hope, though thou hast run, thou hast read. And now
I call the righteous God of heaven to bear me record,
that I have herein sought nothing below the defence of
his unity, mercy, and purity, against the rude and im-
petuous assaults of tradition, press, and pulpit, from
whence I daily hear, what rationally induceth me to
believe, a conspiracy is held by counter-plots, to ob-
struct the exaltation of truth, and to betray evangelical doctrines to idle traditions. But God will rebuke
the winds, and destruction shall attend the enemies of
his anointed.—Mistake me not, we never have dis-
owned a Father, Word, and Spirit, which are *one*, but
men's inventions. 1. Their *trinity* has not so much
as a foundation in the scriptures. 2. Its original was
three hundred years after christianity was in the world.
3. It having cost much blood; in the council of Sir-
mium, Anno 355, it was decreed, "that thenceforth

the controversy should not be remembered, because
the scriptures of God made no mention thereof."[*]
Why then should it be mentioned now with a marana-
tha on all that will not bow to this abstruse opinion.
4. And it doubtless hath occasioned idolatry; witness
the popish images of Father, Son, and Holy Ghost.
5. It scandalizeth Turks, Jews, and infidels, and palpa-
bly obstructs their reception of the christian doctrine.
Nor is there more to be said on the behalf of the other two; for I can boldly challenge any person to give
me one scripture phrase which does approach the doctrine of satisfaction, (much less the name), considering
to what degree it is stretched. Not that we deny, but
really confess, that Jesus Christ, in life, doctrine, death,
fulfilled his father's will, and offered up a most satis-
factory sacrifice; but not to pay God, or help him, (as
otherwise being unable), to save men. And for a justification by an imputative righteousness, whilst not real, it is merely an imagination, not a reality, and therefore rejected; otherwise confest and known to be justifying before God, because *there is no abiding in
Christ's love without keeping his commandments.*
I therefore caution thee in love, of whatsoever tribe,
or family of religion thou mayest be, not longer deceive thyself by the over-fond embraces of human apprehensions for divine mysteries. But rather be informed that God hath bestowed a measure of his grace
on thee and me, to show what is good, that we may
obey and do it; which if thou diligently wilt observe,
thou shalt be led out of all unrighteousness, and in thy
obedience shalt thou receive power to become a son of

[*] Socrat. Schol. An. 365. Conc. Sirm. cap. 25. page. 275.

God; in which happy estate God only ean be known by men, and they know, themselves to be justified before him, whom experimentally to know, by Jesus Christ, is life eternal.

A postscript of animadversions, upon Thomas Vincent's contradictions, delivered in his sermon from 1 John v. 4. at the evening lecture in Spittle-yard; "For whatsoever is born of God, overcometh the world."

DOCTRINE.—"Whatsoever person is born of God, overcometh the world." | "There is a twofold victory; the first complete, the second incomplete."

ANIMAD.—This is as well a contradiction to his text and doctrine, as to common sense. For besides that they neither of them say, "he that is born of God, cannot perfectly overcome the world," but much the contrary; I fain would understand his intention by an incomplete victory. If he means not such a one as is obtained by the slaughter of every individual, but that which only subdues the force, and leads captive their enemies, yet will the victory prove complete; for if they be so far overcome as to be disarmed of farther power to mischief, the dispute is properly determined. But whatsoever is incomplete, is but overcoming, or in the way to victory, and victory is the completing of what was before imperfect.

CONTRADICT. "Such overcome as are born again, who are in Christ, that have cast off the old man, and know a change altogether new." | "Worldly lusts cannot be extirpated out of God's people in this world."

ANIMAD. If sin must have a place in them, how can they be born of God, and have a place in Christ, or cast off the old man, and know a change altogether new?

CONTRADICT. " God's children are the greatest conquerors. Alexander, and Cæsar were conquerors, but these overcome their lusts."

" God's children cannot perfectly overcome the lusts of this world; they sometimes take them captive."

ANIMAD. What strange divinity is this ! That God's people should be conquerors, and yet captives ; overcome the world, and yet be overcome thereby.

CONTRADICT. " Sin may tyrannize over believers."

" But not have dominion; it is in captivity; it is in chains."

ANIMAD. Who is so absolutely injurious and incontrolable, as a tyrant? And notwithstanding that he should have no dominion, but be in captivity, and in chains, at best are Bedlam distinctions, and consequently unworthy of any man's mouth that has a share of common sense.

CONTRADICT. " You must kill, or be killed ; either you must overcome the world, or the world you."

" If ye fight, ye shall overcome."

" Incompletely; he overcomes, when he breaks their force, leads them captive, and puts them into chains; but they are not at all slain, they sometimes take him captive."

ANIMAD. To kill, or be killed, admits no middle way to escape ; yet that both sin and God's children should lead one another captive ; and that he which fights shall overcome, and yet be in danger of being led captive, because completely a conqueror, to me seems very strange doctrine.

However, he goes on to tell them, "Whosoever is born of God, overcometh the lusts of the world, and he that overcometh the lusts of the world, overcomes the devils of hell; God's children have to do with a conquered enemy." Yet he would all this while he understood in an "incomplete sense;" and to excite all to fight for this "incomplete victory," he recommended to their consideration, the excellent rewards of conquerors, that is: "To him that overcometh, will I give to eat of the tree of life, the hidden manna. I will give him a white stone, a new name, power over nations, white raiment; yea, I will make him a pillar in the temple of my God; he shall go no more out, and I will grant him to sit with me in my throne." Admirable privileges, I acknowledge! But are they promised to "incomplete conquerors?" I judge not.

Reader, by this thou mayest be able to give a probable conjecture of the rest. And as I have begun with him and his co-disputants, with them I will end; who, notwithstanding all their boasts and calumnies against us, have so evaded those many opportunities we have offered them by letters, verbal messages, and personal visits, that had they any zeal for their principles, love for their reputation, or conscience in their promises, they would have been induced to a more direct and candid treaty.

But as it hath occasioned the publication of this little treatise, so I am credibly informed, through the too busy and malicious inquisition of some concerning it, (which have amounted to no less than positive reports), it is currently discoursed, "how that a cer-

tain Quaker hath lately espoused the controversy a-
gainst R. F. and therein has perverted the christian religion, to that degree, as plainly to deny Christ's com-
ing-in the flesh;" with much more than was fit to be
said, or is fit to be answered.

But, reader, I shall ask no other judge to clear me
from that most uncharitable accusation; since first I
am altogether unacquainted with R. F. nor ever did
design directly such a thing, being unwilling to seek
more adversaries than what more nearly seek the over-
throw of truth; although I doubt not but this plain and
simple treatise may prove some confutation of his sen-
timents.

And lastly, as concerning Christ; although the slander is not new, yet nevertheless false. For I declare on
the behalf of that despised people, vulgarly called Quakers, the grace of which we testify, hath never taught
us to acknowledge another God than he that is the Father of all things, who fill heaven and earth. Neither to confess another Lord Jesus Christ, than he that
appeared so many hundred years ago, made of a virgin,
like unto us in all things, sin excepted; or any other
doctrine than was by him declared and practised.
Therefore let every mouth be stopped from ever open-
ing more, in blasphemy against God's innocent heritage, who in principle, life and death, bear an unani-
mous testimony for the only true God, true Christ,
and heavenly doctrine, which in their vindication is
openly attested by

WILLIAM PENN.

INNOCENCY

WITH HER OPEN FACE.

PRESENTED

BY WAY OF APOLOGY,

FOR THE BOOK ENTITLED

THE SANDY FOUNDATION SHAKEN.

———ooo———

BY WILLIAM PENN.

———ooo———

"He that uttereth a slander is a fool." Prov. x. 18.
"A false balance is an abomination to the Lord." Prov. xi. 1.

RELIGION, although there can be nothing of greater concernment, nor which doth more essentially import the immortal happiness of men ; yet such is the calamity of the age, that there is not any thing they are less solicitous about, or serious in the prosecution of, vainly imagining it to consist in the implicit subscription to, and verbal confession of men's invented traditions and precepts, whilst they neglect that more orthodox definition of the apostle James, viz. "Pure religion and undefiled before God is, to visit the fatherless, and to keep himself unspotted from the world ;" Jam. i. 17. and instead thereof, believe they are performing the best of services, in sacrificing the reputation, lib-

erty, estate, if not life itself of others to their own tenacious conceptions; because perhaps, though persons
of more virtue, they cannot in all punctillios corres-
pond therewith. How much I have been made an instance must needs be too notorious to any that hold
the least intelligence with common fame, that scarce
ever took more pains to make the proverb good, by
proving herself a liar, than in my concern ; who have
been most egregiously slandered, reviled and defamed
by pulpit, press, and talk, terming me a blasphemer,
seducer, Socinian, denying the divinity of Chiist the
Saviour, and what not? And all this about my late
answer to a disputation with some Presbyterians ; but
how unjustly, it is the business of this short apology to
show, which had not been thus long retarded, if an ex-
pectation first to have been brought upon my examination had not required a suspense. And if I shall ac-
quit myself from the injurious *imputations* of my adversaries, I hope the cry will have an end. To which
purpose, let but my Innocency have your hearing in
her own defence, who, as she never can detract from
her intentions in what she really hath done; so will she
as easily disprove her enemies, in manifesting their accusations to be ficticious. Judge not before you read,
neither believe any further than you see.

I. That which I am credibly informed to be the
greatest reason for my imprisonment, and that noise of
blasphemy, which hath pierced so many ears of late is,
" my denying the divinity of Christ, and divesting him
of his eternal Godhead," which most busily hath been
suggested, as well to those in authority, as malicious-
ly insinuated amongst the people. Wherefore let me
beseech you to be impartial, and considerate in the pe-

rusal of my vindication, which being in the fear of the Almighty God, and the simplicity of scripture dialect presented to you, I hope my innocency will appear beyond a scruple.

The Proverbs, which, as most agree, intend *Christ the Saviour*, speak in this manner: "By me kings reign, and princes decree justice; I (wisdom) lead in the midst of the paths of judgment; I was set up from everlasting;" Prov. viii. 15. 20. 23. to which Paul's words allude: "unto them which are called, (we preach) Christ the power of God, and the wisdom of God." 1 Cor. i. 24. From whence I conclude Christ the Saviour to be God; for otherwise God would not be himself; since if Christ be distinct from God, and yet God's power and wisdom, God would be without his own power and wisdom.—But inasmuch as it is impossible God's power and wisdom should be distinct or divided from himself, it reasonably follows, that Christ, who is that power and wisdom, is not distinct from God, but entirely that very same God.

Next, the prophets, David and Isaiah, speak thus: "The Lord is my light and my salvation." Psal. xxvii. 1.—"I will give thee for a light unto the gentiles." Isa. xlix. 6.—And speaking to the church: "For the Lord shall be thine everlasting life." c. lx. 20.—To which the evangelist adds, concerning Christ: "That was the true light which lighteth every man that cometh into the world." John i. 9.—"God is light, and in him is no darkness at all." 1 John i. 5.— From whence I assert the unity of God and Christ, because, though nominally distinguished, yet essentially the same Divine Light. For if Christ be that Light, and that Light be God, then is Christ God; or if God

9

... ~~~ Light, and that Light be Christ, then is God
Christ. Again: "And the city had no need of the sun,
for the glory of God did lighten it, and the Lamb
(Christ) is the light thereof." Rev. xxi. 23.—By which
the oneness of the nature of these lights plainly appears; for since God is not God without his own glory, and that his glory lightens, (which it could never
do if it were not light,) and that the Lamb, or Christ
is that very same Light, what can follow, but that
Christ the Light and *God the Light* are *one* pure
and eternal Light.

Next, from the word Saviour, it is manifest: "I
even I, am the Lord, and besides me there is no Saviour." Isa. xliii. 11. "And thou shalt know no God
but me, for there is no Saviour besides me." Hos. xiii.
4.—And Mary said, "My spirit hath rejoiced in God
my Saviour." Luke i. 47.—And the Samaritans said
unto the woman, "Now we know that this is indeed
the Christ the Saviour of the world." John iv. 42.—
"According to his grace made manifest by the appear-
ing of our Saviour Jesus Christ." 2. Tim. i. 9, 10.—
Simon Peter "to them that have obtained like pre-
cious faith with us, through the righteousness of God,
and our Saviour Jesus Christ." 2 Pet. i. 1. "For
therefore we suffer reproach because we trust in the
living God, who is the Saviour of all men." 1 Tim.
iv. 10.—"To the Only wise God our Saviour be glory," &c. Jude, ver. 25.

"From which I conclude Christ to be God; for if
none can save, or be styled properly a Saviour but
God, and yet that Christ is said to save, and properly
called a Saviour, it must needs follow, that Christ the
Saviour is God.

Lastly, "In the beginning was the (LOGOS) Word, (which the Greeks sometimes understood for Wisdom and Divine Reason), and the Word was with God, and the Word was God. All things were made by him, and without him was not any thing made that was made." John i. 1, 3. "For by him were all things created that are in heaven, and that are in earth. He is before all things, and by him all things consist." Col. i. 16, 17.—"Upholding all things by the word of his power," &c. Heb. i. 3, 10.—Wherefore I am still confirmed in the belief of *Christ the Saviour's* divinity; for he that made all things, and by whom they consist and are upheld, because before all things; he was not made nor upheld by another, and consequently is God. Now that this LOGOS, or Word that was made flesh, or Christ the light, power, and wisdom of God, and Saviour of men, hath made all things, and is he by *whom they only consist* and are upheld, because he was before them, is most evident from the recited passages of scripture; therefore he was not made, nor is he upheld by any other power than his own, and consequently is truly God.—In short, this conclusive argument for the proof of *Christ the Saviour's being God*, should certainly persuade all sober persons of my innocency, and my adversaries' malice. He that is the everlasting Wisdom, the Divine Power, the true Light, the only Saviour, the creating Word of all things, whether visible or invisible, and their upholder by his own power, is without contradiction, God. But all these qualifications and divine properties are, by the concurrent testimonies of scripture, ascribed to the Lord Jesus Christ. Therefore, without a scruple, I call and believe him really to be the Mighty God,

And for a more ample satisfaction, let but my reply[*] to J. Clapham be perused, in which Christ's divinity and eternity is very fully asserted.

Judge then, impartial readers, (to whom I appeal in this concern) whether my christian, reputation hath not been unworthily traduced; and that those several persons who have been posting out their books against me (whilst a close prisoner), have not been beating the air and fighting with their own shadows, in supposing what I never thought, much less wrote of, to be the intention of my book; and then as furiously have fastened on me their own conceits, expecting I should feel the smart of every blow, who thus far am no ways interested in their heat.

As for my being a Socinian, I must confess I have read of one Socinus, of (that they call) a noble family in Sene in Italy, who about the year 1574, being a young man voluntarily did abandon the glories, pleasures and honors of the great Duke of Tuscany's court at Florence, (that noted place for all worldly delicacies,) and became a perpetual exile for his conscience, whose parts, wisdom, gravity, and just behaviour made him the most famous with the Polonian and Transylvanian churches. But I was never baptized into his name, and therefore deny that reproachful epithet. And if in any thing I acknowledge the verity of his doctrine, it is for the truth's sake, of which, in many things, he had a clearer view than most of his contemporaries. But not therefore a Socinian, any more than a son of the English church, whilst esteemed a Quaker because I justify many of her principles, since the reformation, against the Roman church.

[*] See vol. 2: Guide Mistaken.

II. As for the business of satisfaction, I am prevented by a person whose reputation is generally great amongst the protestants of these nations. For since the doctrine against which I mostly levelled my arguments was, "the impossibility of God's forgiving sin upon repentance, without Christ's paying his justice, by suffering infinite vengeance and eternal death for sins past, present, and to come," he plainly in his late discourse ‡ about Christ's sufferings, against Crellius, acknowledges me no less, by granting, upon a new state of the controversy, 'both the possibility of God's pardoning sins, as debts, without such a rigid satisfaction, and the impossibility of Christ's so suffering for the world;' reflecting closely upon those persons, as 'giving so just an occasion to the churche's adversaries to think they triumph over her faith, whilst it is only over their mistakes, who argue with more zeal than judgment.' Nay, one of the main ends which first induced me to that discourse, I find thus delivered by him, namely, if they did believe Christ came into the world to reform it, 'that the wrath of God is now revealed from heaven against all unrighteousness, that his love which is shown to the world, is to deliver them from the hand of their enemies, that they might serve him in righteousness and holiness all the days of their lives, they could never imagine that salvation is entailed by the gospel upon a mighty confidence, or vehement persuasion of what Christ hath done and suffered for them.'* Thus doth he confess upon my hypothesis, or proposition, what I mainly contend for. And however positively I may reject or deny my adversaries unscriptu-

‡ Stillingfleet contra Crell, page 269, 270, 271, 272, 273, 274.
*Ib. p. 160.

ral and imaginary satisfaction, let all know this, that I
pretend to know no other name by which remission,
atonement, and salvation can be obtained, but Jesus
Christ the Saviour, who is the power and wisdom of
God, what apprehensions soever people may have en-
tertained concerning me.

III. As for justification by an imputed righteousness,
I still say, that whosoever believes in Christ shall have
remission and justification. But then it must be such a
faith as can no more live without works, than a body
without a spirit; Jam. ii. 26; wherefore I conclude,
that true faith comprehends evangelical obedience.
And here the same Dr. Stillingfleet† comes in to my relief, (though it is not wanting), by a plain assertion of
the necessity of obedience, viz. 'Such who make no
other condition of the gospel but believing, ought to
have a great care to keep their hearts sounder than their
heads;' thereby intimating the grand imperfection and
danger of such a notion. And therefore, (God Almighty bears me record), my design was nothing less nor
more, than to wrest those beloved and sin pleasing principles out of the hands, heads, and hearts of people:
that by the fond persuasion of being justified from the
personal righteousness of another, without relation to
their own obedience, they might not sin on upon trust,
till the arrest of eternal vengeance should irrecoverably
overtake them; that all might be induced to an earnest
pursuit after holiness, by a circumspect observance to
God's Holy Spirit, 'without which none shall ever see
the Lord.' And, to shut up my apology for religious
matters, that all may see the simplicity, scripture doctrine, and phrase of my faith, in the most important

† Ib. p. 164, 165, 166.

matters of eternal life, I shall here subjoin a short con+
fession.

I sincerely own, and unfeignedly believe, (by virtue
of the sound knowledge and experience received from
the gift of that holy unction, and divine grace inspired
from on high), in one holy, just, merciful, almighty,
and eternal God, who is the Father of all things; [1
Cor. viii. 5, 6.] that appeared to the holy patriarchs and
prophets of old, at sundry times, and in divers manners. [Heb. i. 1.] And in one Lord Jesus Christ, [1
Cor. viii. 6.] the everlasting wisdom, divine power,
true light, only Saviour and preserver of all, *the same*
one holy, just merciful, 'Almighty, and eternal God,
who in the fulness of time took, and was manifested in
the flesh; [John i. 14. 1 Tim. iii. 16.] At which time
he preached, [and his disciples after him], the everlasting gospel of repentance, and promise of remission
of sins, and eternal life to *all* that heard and obeyed;
[Mat. iv. 17. Luke xxiv. 47.], who said, he that is with
you, in the flesh, shall be in you, by the spirit; and
though he left them [as to the flesh], yet not comfort-
less, for he would come to them again [in the spirit],
[John xiv. 17, 18.] For a little while, and they should
not see him [as to the flesh ;] again, a little while and
they should see him, in the spirit, (John xvi. 16.) For
the Lord, Jesus Christ, is that Spirit, (2 Cor. iii. 17.) a
manifestation whereof is given to every one to profit
withal.—In which Holy Spirit I believe, as the same
Almighty and eternal God, who, as in those times he
ended all shadows, and became the infallible guide to
them that walked therein, by which they were adopt-
ed heirs and co-heirs of glory; (Rom. viii. 14, 17.) so
am I a living witness, that the same holy, just, merci-

ful, Almighty, and eternal God, is now, as then, (after
this tedious night of idolatry, superstition, and human
inventions that hath overspread the world) gloriously
manifested to discover and save from all iniquity, and
to conduct to the holy land of pure and endless peace;
in a word, to tabernacle in men. [Rev. xxi. 3.] And I
also firmly believe, that without repenting and forsa-
king of past sins, and walking in obedience to this
heavenly voice, which would guide into all truth, and
establish there, remission and eternal life can never be
obtained. (Prov. xxviii. 13.) But unto them that fear
his name, and keep his commandments, they, and they
only shall have right unto the tree of life. (Rev. xxii.
14.) For whose name sake I have been made willing
to relinquish and forsake all the vain fashions, enticing
pleasures, alluring honors, and glittering glories of this
transitory world, [Luke xiv. 33.] and readily to accept
the portion of a fool, from this deriding generation, and
become a man of sorrows, and a perpetual reproach to
my familiars. (1 Pet. iv. 14.) Yea, and with the greatest cheerfulness can designate and confirm, with no
less seal, than the loss of whatsoever this doating world
accounts dear, this faithful. confession, having my eye
fixed upon a more enduring substance, and lasting in-
heritance; and being most infallibly assured, that when
time shall be no more, I shall, if faithful hereunto, possess the mansions of eternal life, and be received into
his everlasting habitation of rest and glory.

IV. Lastly it. may not be unreasonable to observe,
that however industrious some, (those dissenters too),
have been to represent me as a person disturbing the
civil peace, I have not violated any truly fundamental
law which relates to external property and good be-

havior; and not to religious apprehensions, it being the
constant principle of myself and friends, to maintain
good works, and keep our consciences void of offence,
paying active or passive obedience, suitable to the
meek example of our Lord Jesus Christ. Nor would
I have any ignorant, how forward I was by messages,
letters, and visits, to have determined this debate in a
sober and select assembly, notwithstanding the rude
entertainment we had met with before. But contrary
to their own appointments our adversaries failed us,
which necessitated me to that defence; and finding the
truth so pressed with slander, I cannot but say I saw
my just call to her relief. But, alas! how have those two
or three extemporary sheets been tost, tumbled, and
torn on all hands, yea, aggravated to a monstrous design, even the subversion of the christian religion,
than which there could be nothing more repungent to
my principle and purpose. Wherefore how very in-
temperate as well as unjust have all my adversaries
been in their revilings, slanders, and defamations?
Using the most approbious terms of "seducer, here-
tic, blasphemer, deceiver, Socinian, Pelagian, Simon
Magus, impiously robbing Christ of his divinity, for
whom the vengeance of the great day is reserved," &c.*
Nor have these things been whispered, but, in one
book and pulpit after another, have more or less been
thundered out against me, as if some bull had lately
arrived from Rome; and all this acted under the foul
pretence of zeal and love to Jesus Christ, whose meek
and gentle example always taught it for a principal

*See T. Vincent's late railing piece against the Quakers, also
T. Danson's and Dr. Owen's.

10

mark of true christianity, to suffer the most outrage-
ous injuries, but never to return any.—Nay, if my adversaries would but be just and constant to themselves,
how can they offer to conspire my destruction upon a
religious ground, who either are themselves under a
present limitation, or have been formerly by the Papists.
Tell me, I pray, did Luther,* that grand reformer,
whom you so much reverence, justly demand from the
emperor at the diet of Worms, where he was summon-
ed to appear, that none should sit judge upon his doctrines but the scripture, and in case they should be
cast, that no other sentence should be passed upon him,
than what Gamaliel offered to the Jewish council, "if
it were not of God it would not stand." And if you
will not censure him who first of all arraigned the
christian world (so-called) at the bar of his private
judgment), that had so many hundred years soundly
slept, without so much as giving one considerable shrug
or turn, during that tedious winter night of dark apos-
tacy), but justify his proceedings, can you so furiously
assault others? But above all, you, who refuse con-
formity to others, and that have been writing these
eight years of liberty of conscience, and take it at this
very season by an indulgent connivance; what preg-
nant testimonies do you give of your unwillingness to
grant that to others you so earnestly beg for yourselves? Doth it not discover your injustice, and plainly express what only want of power hinders you to
act? But of all protestants in general I demand, do you
believe that persecution to be christian in yourselves,
that you condemned for antichristian in the Papists?
You judged it a weakness in their religion, and is it a

* Coun. Trent. p. 14.

cogent argument in yours? Nay, is it not the readiest way to enhance and propagate the reputation of what you would depress? If you were displeased at their assuming an infalliability, will you believe it impossible in yourselves to err? Have Whitaker, Reynolds, Laud, Owen, Baxter, Stillingfleet, Poole, &c. disarmed the Romanists of these inhuman weapons, that you might employ them against your inoffensive countrymen? Let the example and holy precepts of Christ dissuade you, who " came not to destroy, but save;" and soberly reflect upon his equal law " of doing as you would be done unto." Remember I have not dethroned a divinity, subverted faith, made void obedience, nor frustrated the hope of an eternal recompense; much less have I injured your persons, or in any thing deviated from that THEOS- ENTHETOS and SUNTERESIS, or holy principle, so much insisted on by philosophers and lawyers, as the original of good laws, and life. No, your own consciences shall advocate on my behalf. Let it suffice, then, that we who are nick-named Quakers, have, under every revolution of power and religion, been the most reviled, contemned, and persecuted, as if God indeed " had set us forth in these last days as a spectacle to the world, to angels, and to men ;" 1 Cor. iv. 9. and treated as if, by being what we are, our common right and interst in human societies were forfeited. Neither accept that for a true measure of our life and doctrines, which hath been taken by the ill will or ignorance of others ; but rather make an impartial examination, that what you judge may be from what you know, not from what you hear at second hand ; and then we shall as little question your just opinion of our innocency, as we have too much

been made sensible of the sad effects that follow an ignorant and unadvised zeal. For so monstrously fond
are some of their persuasions, and doating on the pat-
rons of them, that they seldom have discretion, much
less religious disires to consider how true or false another religion is, or what may be the consequences of
its toleration; but with a fury, not inferior to their ignorance, cry crucify, crucify; and pharasee-like, out
of pretence of honor and service done to God Almighty, and the memory of his holy prophets, stick not to
persecute his beloved Son, and righteous servants.
So cruel, blind, and obstinate is persecution. Be therefore advised in the words of that meek example Jesus
Christ, call not for fire any more; let the tares grow
with the wheat; neither employ that sword any more,
which was commanded to be sheathed so many hundred years ago; (suppose we were enemies to the true
religion; but have a care you are not upon one of
Saul's errands to Demaseus, and helping the mighty
against God and his Anointed;) and rather choose by
fair and moderate debates, not penalties ratified by im-
perial decrees, to determine religious differences. So
will you at least obtain tranquility, which may be called a civil unity. But if you are resolved severity
shall take its course, in this, our case can never change,
nor happiness abate, for no human edict can possibly
deprive us of his glorious presence, who is able to
make the most dismal prisons so many receptacles of
pleasure, and whose heavenly fellowship doth unspeak-
ably replenish our solitary souls with divine consola-
tion; by whose holy, meek, and harmless spirit I have
been taught most freely to forgive, and not less earnestly to solicit the temporal and eternal good of all my
adversaries. Farewell. WILLIAM PENN.

A QUESTIONARY POSTSCRIPT.

Where doth the scripture say, that Christ suffered an eternal death, and infinite vengeance? For did not Christ rise the third day? And is not infinite vengeance and eternal death without end? And doth not God say he was well pleased with his Son before his death? And was not his offering acceptable? And did not the apostle say, that the saints were accepted in Christ that was God's beloved? And this was after Christ died and rose; and God was said to be well pleased with his Son, both before he suffered, in his suffering, after he suffered, though displeased with those that caused him to suffer.

CPSIA information can be obtained at www.ICGtesting.com
Printed in the USA
BVOW021813101012

302640BV00006B/259/A

9 781104 505172